Little Pebble™

WHAT LIVING THINGS NEED

Living Things Need
Light

by Karen Aleo

PEBBLE
a capstone imprint

Little Pebble is published by Pebble
1710 Roe Crest Drive, North Mankato, Minnesota 56003
www.mycapstone.com

Library of Congress Cataloging-in-Publication Data
Names: Aleo, Karen, author.
Title: Living things need light / by Karen Aleo.
Description: North Mankato, Minnesota : Pebble, [2019] | Series: Little Pebble. What living things need | "Pebble is published by Capstone." | Audience: Ages 5-7. | Audience: K to grade 3.
Identifiers: LCCN 2019006176| ISBN 9781977108869 (hardcover) | ISBN 9781977110367 (pbk.) | ISBN 9781977108906 (ebook pdf)
Subjects: LCSH: Life (Biology)--Juvenile literature. | Biochemistry--Juvenile literature. | Light--Physiological effect--Juvenile literature. | Sunshine--Juvenile literature.
Classification: LCC QH309.2 .A4425 2019 | DDC 572--dc23
LC record available at https://lccn.loc.gov/2019006176

Editorial Credits
Anna Butzer, editor; Bobbie Nuytten, designer;
Kelly Garvin, media researcher; Kathy McColley, production specialist

Photo Credits
iStockphoto/ori-artiste, 21; Shutterstock: AlinaMD, 5, liseykina, 13, Lynn Yeh, 7, Mikael Hjerpe, 17, Peredn'iankina, 9, Singkham, cover, TinnaPong, 19, Unberrer, 15, wawritto, 11

Printed and bound in China.
1671

Table of Contents

Light

Good morning.

Do you see the sun?

It gives off light and heat.

Plants need light.

It helps them grow.

Light helps animals see.

Plants Need Light

Plants get light from the sun.

They use light to make food.

Leaves take in light.

The light turns into energy.

Plants use energy
to make food.

Light helps plants grow.

Plants need light

to stay alive.

Animals Need Light

Many animals are awake
during the day.
Light helps animals see.

Animals need to be warm.

See the snake?

It is being warmed
by the sunlight. *Hiss!*

People Need Light

Sunlight is good for people.

Sunlight has vitamin D.

It helps us grow strong bones.

Can you feel the sun's light?
It helps keep people warm.

Glossary

energy—the strength to do active things without getting tired

grow—to get bigger in size

heat—a kind of energy that makes things hot or warm

need—to require something; you need food, shelter, and air to stay alive

vitamin D—a substance needed for good health; vitamin D can come from the sun

Read More

Bell, Samantha. *Sunlight*. My World of Science. Ann Arbor, MI: Cherry Lake Publishing, 2018.

Higgins, Nadia. *Busy, Busy Leaves*. My First Science Songs. Minneapolis: Cantata Learning, 2017.

Robertson, Charmaine. *All About Sunlight*. Rosen Real Readers: Stem and Steam Collection. New York: Rosen Classroom, 2016.

Internet Sites

Education.com: Photosynthesis Worksheets and Printables
https://www.education.com/worksheets/photosynthesis/

Fact Monster: What Plants Need to Live and Grow
https://www.factmonster.com/videos/what-plants-need-to-live-and-grow

Critical Thinking Questions

1. How do plants use light?
2. Where do living things get light from?
3. How do animals use light?

Index